WITCHERY

ELIZABETH L. HODGES

MADHAT PRESS
ASHEVILLE, NORTH CAROLINA

MadHat Press
MadHat Incorporated
PO Box 8364, Asheville, NC 28814

Copyright © 2016 Elizabeth L. Hodges
All rights reserved

ISBN 978-1-941196-27-4
Library of Congress Control Number: 2016902398

Text by Elizabeth L. Hodges
Book and cover design by Kevin Romoser
Cover photo © Clark A. Hodges, Jr.

Artwork copyright © Ed Ruscha
Courtesy of the Artist and Gagosian Gallery

www.MadHat-Press.com

First Printing

Nothing Landscape

Ed Ruscha
1987
acrylic on canvas
54 × 120 inches
© Ed Ruscha. Courtesy of the Artist and Gagosian Gallery

○|○ PRINCIPLES OF DESIRE

White Noise	5
Warrior	6
Changeling	7
Birthday	8
Three Questions	9
Painful with Extension	10
Hold those things close that bruise the skin	12
Millennium	14
Genesis	15

○○|○○ MIND

Obscure Longings	21
5:37 p.m.	22
Business Trips	23
Accidental	24
Life goes on in the deep, dark forest	25
Secret	27
Fortune Teller	28
Personification of numbers: an explanatory title	29
Mystic	31

○ SPIRIT

Cycle of the Moon	39
Blindmen and Beggars	40
Pale Fish	41
La Tarantella	42
Needle	43
The Knife	44
Snatches of Conversation	45
Carpathus	46
Daedalus	47

○ SOUL

Pilgrimage	55
Hitchhiker	56
Writing it down for the doctor	57
Burden	58
Malady	59
Finally Remembering	61
Amarga Dulce	62
Being Still	63
Blue Ridge	64

for Ruby Norris

...LET THE BONES DANCE WHICH THOU HAS BROKEN.

                                    from Psalms 51

HIS OWN FACE IN THE MIRROR, HIS OWN HANDS, SURPRISED HIM ON EVERY OCCASION.

                                  "Funes, the Memorious"
                                  Jorge Luis Borges

PRINCIPLES OF DESIRE

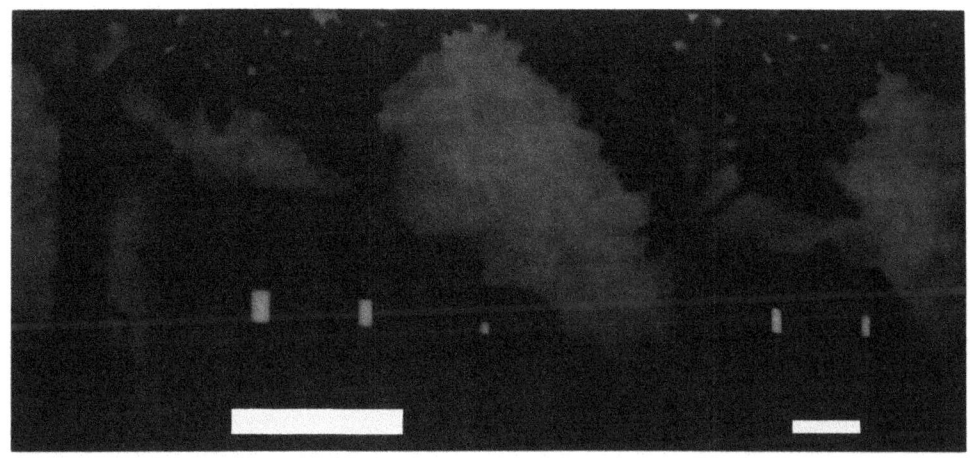

Strong, Healthy

Ed Ruscha
1987
acrylic on canvas
54 × 120 inches
© Ed Ruscha. Courtesy of the Artist and Gagosian Gallery

WHITE NOISE

Restless,
I lie in bed in apprehension of the wind
and when it comes
I satisfy myself with childish night terrors;
the willow tree blew down
when I was four,
I loved the willow tree more
than anything.
In the distance, waves
claim the range of notes from
high to low and blend in almost perfect
crashes on the shore, a forever roar
in the dark that paces the past with me
as if the past were the cottage floor.
Everything is
still until my cry
interrupts your breathing. I
wrap my leg around your thigh and beg you to hold me
close enough to block the endless sea,
the sound that fills all frequencies.

WARRIOR

Among the lichen, green
with the dark wood of giant trees,
grey with shadows on velvet floors
among the leaves; amidst
the moss, here is this crimson spore, fruit
that breeds more.

Alone it waits for what moves
in flickers, an alien face,
the rebel guerrillas.

CHANGELING

Your bare chest so pale,
father-mist rising. The sound:
chopping wood/silence.
And all around the forest plays a game
of coaxing tongues from us—always the same
twig, always the same
carp mouthing the pond's surface,
always my desire,
always your labor.

BIRTHDAY

White/white walls,
rose clay pots,
saucers to catch the overspill,
a watercolor bathed in artificial light;
you give your candle spirit up
for substance.

The one place to which you come home.

The one scotch in Waterford crystal.

The one woman who sits at your window sill,
a flower you never pick.

THREE QUESTIONS

The moon was full two nights ago.
Now, I know. I almost missed
its waxing, my mind on other things: the continuum
of an agony, a puzzle with no riddle, a feather
Dionysus wore in his hair once. Feather, labyrinth,
skull and bone: which occupies the largest room
of my despair? Two nights ago,
the moon was full and unless I had seen the
two bright spots that were your cheeks, the primal
glow reflected there, I would have missed it.
But, I saw your longing (an expression too rare)
and then through the mist that would be clouds,
there was the moon. "It's full?" I asked. You
didn't answer. "Are you still there?"
The word was "yes," I think you said.

PAINFUL WITH EXTENSION

In all the trees, light hesitated
before it filtered through the leaves and fell on your shoulders,
camouflaging your sweater,
darker with the shadows
than the ground. The morning rays avoided
your face, landing instead on objects. Mica
in the gravel under our bicycles
gathered what it could from the open spaces,
the tiniest trace of quartz a signal
to mark our way through the poplar groves.

We pedaled for three hours and returned to our room.

Even after a hot bath,
your legs ached when I massaged them
over and over,
careful with the calves,
trying not to bruise them further,
kneading the rest more vigorously.
Remember this morning, I think to myself,
please, more than anything else,
this place
that you have put on already

without knowing.

And you turn on your back,
not an invitation to caress,
but because I'm through,
and you slowly exercise your legs,
afternoon sun making them appear as thin saplings
against the window,
tracing the lines, your grimace
in the discipline.

HOLD THOSE THINGS CLOSE THAT BRUISE THE SKIN

I cry at last
the blows
of those curled up in balls.
My frame
racked out in corner posts;
my heart,
sour gall,
moves up my throat.

A row of men stand by to see
this fevered bruise;
you must know me.

I've lost myself in voids of rage.

You must know me.

Just say my name.

Your face is there on different shoulders;
each face a smile,
each smile grows stronger on my sores.

I'm worn with wondering which one is you
to hold me close,
to see me through.

You must know me;
just say my name.

Your voices echo all the same.
Your voices chorus, "all is well."
Your row of hands caress the air.

MILLENNIUM

An egg cracks. The thin veined petals unfold.
A pretty woman opens a box and chooses
the gold she will wear today. A closet door stands
ajar, a full length mirror tells what they are:
silk tie, pressed lapels, sleek thigh, perfume Arpel.
Someone downstairs calls their names; the sound
floats, hovers. Their backs are turned, out the
window eyes roam. The sun in the sky hangs
low today. A voice is impatient. It stays that way.

GENESIS

Coming together are two orbs of light, now
touching, the explosion a nova. Intensely
she burns and her core is heavy and black.
It was this land he first touched with his
belly when he slithered aground to stay. And
the night sky is a reflection of the water.
The air feeds her longing. Without fear,
she holds what the ocean yields. They.
They are moving along parallel lines that
meet somewhere in the future. Furnaces
rage all night to extinguish the darkness,
steam rises from the adobe of their foundation.

MIND

Name

Ed Ruscha
1987
acrylic on canvas
59 × 145½ inches
© Ed Ruscha. Courtesy of the Artist and Gagosian Gallery

OBSCURE LONGINGS

It is not detachment she wants. It is
what she would consider a sane mind; the
sharing of a joint in front of a stone
fireplace without her thoughts drifting to the empty
beaches, the peopleless out-of-season houses,
the madmen who wander through the scrub
pine in the rain (in her childhood fantasies) looking
for contentedness in order to destroy it with a whack.
It is not an inability to face facts of
some despair she longs for or to replace
understanding with naiveté; it is that she wants
to close out for a while the banging shutters, the
worlds beyond the burning driftwood, a piercing light
through the fog at the edge of the dune. She
wants to reflect only those visible
things and not confuse issues with the pain they bring.

5:37 P.M.

Not many thirty-five cent original price Anatole France
paperbacks around these days.
It is a clue to the person.
Smelling like someone else's bookshelf, the glue binding
no longer effective, the crease down the cover.
He didn't answer when I came home.
I bought him the book. On women's wounds and where they lead
(red death, black net death, light my cigarette death).
He wasn't napping in the other room.
It's probably important that he left it on page 86, face
down, that the earmarked corner smells like oranges, that
the skins are in a dish beside the bed.

BUSINESS TRIPS

Just inside the door she sees a scarf dropped carelessly
on the floor and as she steps into the room
she thinks, "He's back," shows no apparent excitement.
She calmly bends down and picks it up, examines
the weave, reads the label. "He's been abroad," she
muses as she carefully smoothes the soft cloth and
hangs it on the coat rack. She leans against
the wall, feels the warm air from the heater around
her feet and calves, closes her eyes, and
rubs her forehead with her thumbs and fingers.
Silence. It is so quiet. If she could just
be sure that he hadn't heard the clicking
of the door, she would stand there forever, not
moving, one small frame her existence—she could endure
eternity in her plaid wool coat and leggings. She
is suddenly too warm and too alive. Her stomach growls.
She rubs her eyes. Stuffs her mittens in her hat. And cries.

ACCIDENTAL

In the coffee shop, she is sure he recognizes her face. She
has been over the night again and again in her mind when
she finds the space too closed in. If you have ever felt
sorry, then you know how weighty the head can be. She doesn't
remember much except the lights and her own voice sounding
unreal and horrible. But that is enough to repeat itself.
He turns to speak. Where has he seen her? He doesn't see
the scars, doesn't take in the shaking cup of coffee or her handbag
pressed against her chest. She has always felt as if she
had been driving, as if she were the cause instead of
the effect. He remembers. She puts a dollar beside the cup
and rushes to catch the 8:30 bus. She rides one stop beyond
her own and walks back. A habit she's gotten into.

LIFE GOES ON IN THE DEEP, DARK FOREST

The house is made of ginger cake
is five stories high
is home to twenty families
none of which have children.
There is a resident witch,
the landlord,
who lets the spun sugar collect in corners
for the mice.
Times are hard,
the tenants say
as they climb up the stairs,
go down again into the basement
to wash their clothes
and hang then to dry
on licorice lines.
Bored Mrs. Greenwich looks
outside:
the children play hopscotch on the sidewalk
occasionally marking the score
in the pink icing on the corner stone,
carefully wiping their fingers
on their handkerchiefs.

Mrs. Greenwich's face,
distorted by the rock candy window panes,
looks young again.
It is getting too dark to play.
The children run away home.
The landlord preheats his oven
to bake new roof tiles
and wonders why his world
couldn't stay the same.

SECRET

She can't write it down because it was years
ago and anything she says now would
betray the simplicity of that moment.
Even in her dreams, when she approaches
what seems to be the answer, a blinding
white light falls like a curtain on her
premonitions. To think it would still
bother her after all these years. It
is like imagining that we dream of
falling because we once slept in trees. It
is like saying genius is only born of a
deviate mind. So she sits—chewing her
pencil and staring at the even blue
lines and thinking perfect thoughts before
she can bring herself to write characters
on the page. Never (it is so impossible)
would she want to see anything of herself there,
acting on the stage.

FORTUNE TELLER

A wizened woman sits by the road
saying, "Put down in symbols what passes the soul."
Hair the texture of thistle down;
texture is something woven round her shoulders
as there she sits all brown and grey,
says she, "Put down in numbers what you say."
Two people meet under her watchful eye,
another orbits by night,
encircling the pair,
for a moment three, then two objects again.
Love and lust join by the sea that rushes the shore
where the vigil is kept. Gone is gone—
it slipped away, this thing that shines in her eyes by day.
A wizened woman sits drinking tea,
reads the leaves,
says what the leaves don't read.

PERSONIFICATION OF NUMBERS:
AN EXPLANATORY TITLE

one
tottering along on new legs fawn-like
three times three is not what it seems
white-haired boy

two
cupid falls victim to her curious arrows
lessons unfold petals and flame
baffling papilionid

three
as he paws the ground, smoke circles his head
he leads and is led by the calf ring in his nostrils
alone in a field of poppies

four
sagacious born weaving seeds into blossom
her pale beauty is saluted in temples and sanctuaries
Arietis sends her stars

five
from a cracked cup lake froth spills

this man image of mother and daughter fantasies
through seedlings he drinks deep

six
tangled in the coattails of a wiser fool
his red eyes dribble ale onto a patchy beard
where horns make merry

seven
his knowledge spirals into a kingdom
numbers form a circle to hear his magical weapon
weary and weak, he loves

eight
in the land of Roister Doister
the needle was lost with his direction
a cur backwith and heretoafter

nine
satan's beard billows in Olympian style
easy words that stick in his mouth shine kind through his eyes
he is their wise

MYSTIC

Slowly it melts
over three matches,
liquid numbers:
one for the innocent,
the womb knowledge,
the regression;
two for the flame
blue and white,
the escape to beauty;
three for the body,
taut and knowing,
the veins running
dark
under the skin
to the heart.
I have watched
what you have told me
to watch,
counting the seconds
until you nod
like white magic.
I remember candles
on a cake.

I remember tall grass and
beetles on my bare legs.
I remember the sky
at night,
the shower of stars.
All these things
I will never forget;
course through my memory
like wine
like tests.

SPIRIT

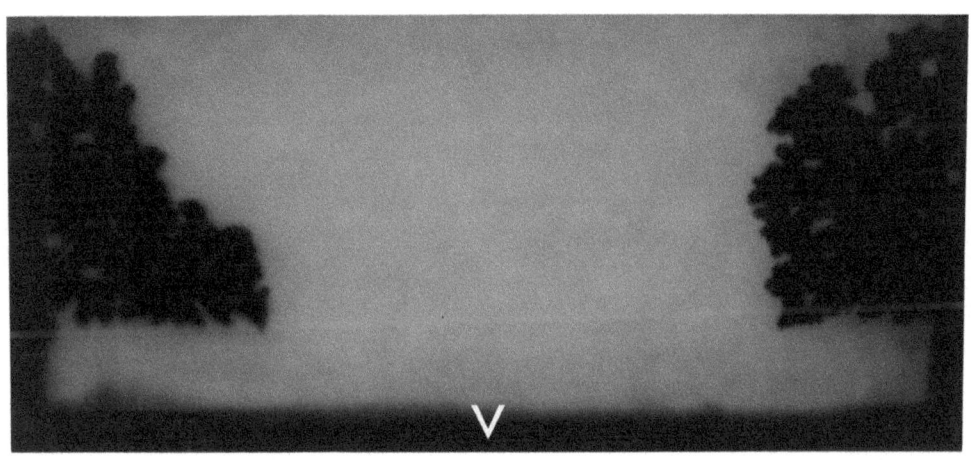

Victory

Ed Ruscha
1987
acrylic on canvas
40 × 90 inches
© Ed Ruscha. Courtesy of the Artist and Gagosian Gallery

CYCLE OF THE MOON

How red the blood
red
the stream
of consciousness
flowing
along
her legs
the holes
two fine
round holes
gape open
dry
her face is pale
of thoughts
the sap
bright red
runs down
her legs
her neck
is strained
veins and bloodless
she doesn't know
it leaves
her cold.

BLINDMEN AND BEGGARS

The dogs are a gift from bombed villages
where even the streets are unfit for dogs.
They look for scraps of the explosion
in the disciplined insanity of rejoicing.
Their hungry eyes see through the layers of wool and flesh
and count the ribs of poverty.
It is bones they know.
And emptiness.
What is music when it reflects
their own long howls at the moon
and they remember the search cry they once carried?
Now, they sing on concrete corners
for their supper
and watch the tongue of the butcher
and wait
for another bombing.

PALE FISH

Behind the day and its blood bait of turtles,
A fisherman stands straining with his net
And the ghost of water creatures.

He knows the monsters,
Looks them straight in the eye,
And thinks of gods and God.

At night, the moon reminds him of their stare.

Ancient fears crawl his skin like scales.

LA TARANTELLA

I will only die with time,
the dance
is but
a paroxysm
of the mind.
The clock
keeps rhythm
a constant
droll reminder
that the waltz is mine
the tango mine
the rock
and roll
are only mine.
Glad partner
join with me
the hands of faces
numbered races
and feel the footwork
precise paces
joined with arrows
of knowing graces
growing old,
growing old.

NEEDLE

The most dangerous of all is the puncture wound.
Clean it well.
This I learned from a *Red Cross First Aid Manual*.
I have always believed in instruction.
Looking through the *New York Times* science section,
I happen onto an article on melanoma,
see each pore as a puncture,
each opening into the body an area of potential invasion.
These days,
there is no more instruction about well-being.
What you believe is instruction.
There is valium in the tap water.
There is a way to control whole populations
with the use of electro-magnetic energy.
This sometimes coincides with the cycle of the moon.
Some feel we are still a primitive people.
I, for one, practice ritual.
There is a case I carry in my purse.
Each night, I take it out, unwrap the contents from their felt cloth.
Each night, I perform one small act of defiance.
It is not what you think.
I am careful and clean.
It is for those who believe
what they don't know won't hurt them
to worry.

THE KNIFE

A stub of arm
lies comfortable in his lap;
there is no hand.
Though I've seen
detached limbs,
sleek with the precision
of a surgeon's weapon,
floating bored
with no direction.
The hand is there.
His hand
holding a subway strap.
His arm
lies peaceful in his lap.

SNATCHES OF CONVERSATION

It is becoming easier and easier to talk with people;
the words I hear beginning to reflect belief. The deities
have changed. Become familiar. More often
I find in myself what others are saying. A woman
stood up and said, I am you, but we're not ready. A man
whispers in my ear, I am tired, but ready to move. Two
people in a cabin stoke the fire and say, patience, and,
are you ready for this? Ready. Waiting. Listening.
Holding onto the constant hum of sounds that soothe, refusing
to repeat obscenities, atrocities, mutations of the language.
The world is a gentle place too long having been bombarded
with verbiage. It is what I hear silently, in the end,
that becomes important. The conviction
passed from hand to hand at the street corner,
in the factory, at the market. The determination
in folded slips of touch. Endurance in the steady rapidity
of the heart, stilled and quiet within its fragile cage.

CARPATHUS

Most of the time, too caught up in immediacy, we move
through the streets without seeing. Old woman, however,
you remind me of a face I've seen in dreams. In sleep,
guided by the hands of clocks, I locate the landscape
and there you are. Transformed, sitting on a now ethereal bench,
the same bright scarf over your hair, the same stalk
of beautiful dried weed in your hand, the same tendency
to stare abstractly through me. But in my dreams, our eyes,
the same color brown, meet and fix that instant
before our spirits traverse in different directions.
Now, I go to buy fruit. You rest a while.

DAEDALUS

It is dancing to the right beat
of an animal skin stretched tightly over a hollow gourd,
bare brown chest glistening with the fire,
hands holding for dear life onto the wings
made from the bright tail feathers of birds, this color for luck in
    hunting,
that for fertility.
All the time, the arms are trying to move with the grace of an
    eagle,
trying to lift the weight of gravity encased in flesh,
trying to fly.

It is this foot pulling off the ground in rhythm,
coming back down,
that knee pulled almost to the chin,
arms working,
feathers fanning the fire,
leaping,
coming back down.

It is jumping high,
a silhouette momentarily above the ring of noise,
suspended in air

with that frightening face of realizing
balance,
landing,
garishly marked for magic,
preparing to rise again.

SOUL

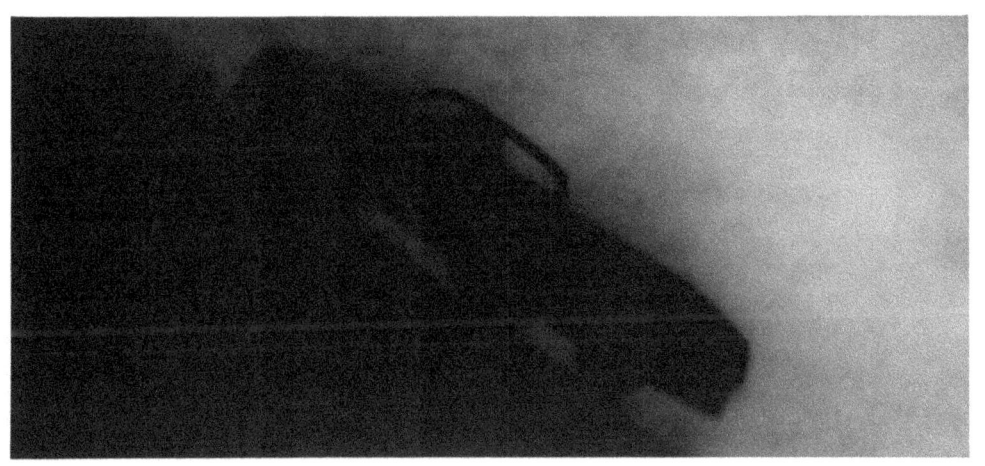

Uphill Driver

Ed Ruscha
1986
acrylic on canvas
54 × 120 inches
© Ed Ruscha. Courtesy of the Artist and Gagosian Gallery

PILGRIMAGE

Too tired for the journey, they wrap their most delicate things
in newspaper and tape the boxes closed. Among the trash,
she finds a clipping she has saved for such a day as this. They
read each even line, side by side on the Afghan rug before
it is rolled, tied with heavy rope, and placed away.
Later, on the trip, octagonal shapes, orange and red,
keep forming in the ice on the windshield in front of her eyes.
He takes her hand and traces the crystal forms with her finger.
It is like salt, he says, don't look back. How many times
they had left the looming figures behind, the old ways,
the knowing nothing of knowing. They now know looking back
is no longer a question, and, yet, in the wind around them,
there is always the temptation, the sound of a child
crying in the corner.

HITCHHIKER

Blew on his dice
and gave him a ride
through a quarter of the state
without knowing his game.

Then, his bony fingers
explored me
like I was part of
his asphalt world and from scene to scene
he laughed and showed me
his torn-down, broken-toy landscape
until I dropped him off.

Selling my car
was a trick
(I picked up) to prolong our separation
but secretly
I knew
one day
he'd be the driver.

WRITING IT DOWN FOR THE DOCTOR

Today, my hand trembles when I touch words
vaguely reminiscent of emotion:
"sunlight that glowed slightly purple" frightens
me as surely as a day-old infant
is startled by some rough wool, textures
being too much for the simple souls of
babies. And myself. Just come back from death,
just yesterday having swallowed my portion
of the River Lethe like a dutiful
spirit, I am forgetful when I speak.
Do I ramble? You said only along
a slender thread that holds me together.
Then, it must have preceded me, this thread
that holds me together must be the stitch
of others too. Love? No, it would be wasted,
taste like salt, the skin, a tear, the river.
What I remember is the
fog that was emotion, the gossamer
covering that made me human; before
the numbness of Elysian Fields, before
fearful reflections showed me uncovered.

BURDEN

She will never be well oh
no oh no in the bed the mounds
of blankets make her forget
her body underneath it all
and if she could just go
away for a while like to
an island but not have to
go really physically if
she could just move weightless
unencumbered by what troubles
her if there were just hot
springs in her mind if she
could just slip into some
thing more comfortable and
not feel so oh no damn guilty.

MALADY

There are others more victimized;
who bleed internally,
subtle expressions on their faces,
but they should beware
the clot that grows inside,
like a gyre, ever spreading. I am
wary of my own (oh so graceful)
attempt at smiling malcontent.
My sorrow rose, figure from a whirlpool that
survived one ocean hell, then two.
I was the victim. I loved the sea
breeze as it wound its current
into something terrible;
the spit of salt
as I went down
was element enough
to reunite myself with self.
I held the sadness as it turned to
foam: posed my ascent from
beneath the surface where darkness
loomed.

There are others more victimized

who bleed and never know the size
of their own torture.

FINALLY REMEMBERING

*For Thelma Elizabeth Brown Ramsey
and Emma Louise Hedrick Hodges*

Yes. Blue suits the dead.
I only wish I had looked closer
to remember
the cut of dress;
they put her in
a solid walnut casket polished to such a finish
no one dared touch the wood
lest she carry their prints
into the grave.
There should be a certain reverence
for beauty. Alive,
even in my dreams, she rises again
from a long illness;
alive, she held me to her breasts,
the soft warm flesh immediate
through her cotton dress,
and smelled of nothing,
delicious nothingness.

AMARGA DULCE

Cartegena 1978

It is so relaxed here sitting under the coconut palms
and waiting for my coffee. I cannot think about the eleven-
year-old boy who played in the ocean with me and asked me to
take him home to America. I cannot think about my friend, the
doctor, who bleeds his patients for a seat at the head table
of the hotel worker's party. I cannot think about the woman
with swollen legs or the man without them, so careful they are
in the streets, so deliberately they move. I cannot think
about cardboard shelter torn down to a rubble, to a flat heap
for banana skins, to make the view more pleasant for *gringos*.
I cannot think about a motorcycle ride so close to the sea that
surf sprays my lips with the sun that is emerging there. I
cannot think. Yet, when my coffee does not come, I write,
with no purpose, the sad and sweet of the day, already filled
to the brim, as if it were mine.

BEING STILL

When we found them in the shed, behind the rollback
desk with its legs gnawed through to the splintered wood, pale

in contrast to the veneer, when we found them there,
enmeshed in spiders' webs and the kind of dust that

dirt and age make, we thought they might be useful in
some fashion. Four wooden bowls. Shaped on different

wheels these shallow ovals, but nested in their stack
from large to small, secured by rings of settling grime

to so become a set. Tonight, I lie upon you,
awkwardly fitting the jut of my hip bone into

the crevice between your thighs, at rest for, what seems
it could be, a very long time. We settle in

a buffered place. Cobwebs form almost overnight;
the corners we swept and cleaned must again

be tended. But, now, in the roughed-out hollows of
our bed, we lie the fallow forms of duration.

BLUE RIDGE

In the mountains, there is more than slate
and red clay. There are more vivid images
than this: the sunset and twisted limbs
of pear trees against the sky. There is
tobacco. A stone chimney. Old clapboard
place. An ice house. Caverns of time
and space. Slowly, the narrow road winds
into the hills, the arbor of trees comforting
in their natural confines, and, then, with
just one turn, the ceiling disappears and
I am engulfed in a past that has no dimensions.
Figures bob between the rows in the field,
shadows against the wall. Once, there was
a cabin beside the chimney; already it is
buried with its persona. Hand tools
and bottles. Songs in the wind. As it
whistles through the broken windows of
the ice house, I listen from where I stand
rigid in the corner. I have reached the edge.
I am afraid of what the dark might hold
if I lose my footing. Sighs in the wood. *Fear
is for the unknown. You have nowhere else*

to go. There is no place you would rather be. You cannot rest unless you be here. Another shadow that will pass.

ACKNOWLEDGMENTS

"White Noise," "Carpathus," and "Millennium,"
The Boston Monthly

"Changeling," *The Connecticut Poetry Review*

"Birthday," *Aspect*

"5:37 p.m.," *The New Virginia Review*

"Business Trips," *The Hollins Critic*

"Personification of numbers: an explanatory title,"
Intro 6: Life As We Know It

"Blindmen and Beggars," *World Guild Magazine*

"Pale Fish" and "Amarga Dulce," *Real Paper*

"Needle" and "Snatches of Conversation,"
The Greenfield Review

"Hitchhiker," *Poets On: Turning Points*

"Being Still," *Poets On: Surviving*

"Blue Ridge," *The North American Review*

"Obscure Longings," *Runes*

"The Knife," *Zymbol*

"Secret," *Mudfish*

Elizabeth L. Hodges is the editor/publisher of *St. Petersburg Review* and *Springhouse Journal*. She has published work in *The Connecticut Poetry Review*, *The Greenfield Review*, *The New Virginia Review*, *The North American Review*, and *Ploughshares* among others. *Witchery* is her first book of poetry.